MW01611781

to Football

(For Anyone Who Wants to Understand America's Favorite Sport)

by Randall D. Schultz

Edited by Virginia L. Schultz

Book Bites™

Published by
Schultz Communications
9412 Admiral Nimitz NE
Albuquerque, NM 87111
(505) 822-8222

Contents

ISBN 0-9634621-0-5

Introduction

Each fall, millions of football fans become glued to their television sets every weekend to watch football. Unfortunately, if you don't  understand the game you'll find it difficult to enjoy and virtually impossible to talk about. And asking questions during a game is guaranteed to get you "shushed" by most fanatical football fans.

This guidebook is designed to make your life more bearable during football season — which begins in late summer and continues all the way until the Super Bowl in late January. By understanding the basics of the game, you'll have a greater appreciation for this exciting sport. With any luck, you may even become a genuine football fan.

NOTE: In this book we focus on professional football, as played in the National Football League (NFL).

The Basics

Football is a game played by two teams, each having 11 players on the field. The basic idea in football is to control possession of the ball so that points may be scored. This is done by moving the ball down the field using running or passing plays. As in most sports, the team with the most points at the end of the game wins.

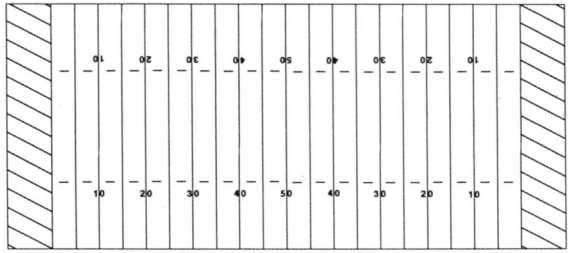

The football field is sometimes called a *gridiron* because someone (probably a man) thought its pattern of lines resembled the cooking utensil used to broil foods.

The football itself is an oval-shaped ball made of leather that's inflated with air. The odd shape of the ball makes it relatively easy to throw. It also makes it bounce funny — making the game especially interesting when a player *fumbles* (drops the ball during play). When a football is fumbled, nobody knows where it will end up.

Offense and Defense

The team with possession of the ball is the *offense*, or *offensive team.* The team without the ball is the *defense,* or *defensive team.*

The offensive team has four plays to move the ball 10 yards down the field. (The defensive team tries to prevent the offensive team from moving the ball down the field.)

If the offensive team successfully moves the football 10 yards in four plays or less, it keeps the ball. Otherwise, the defensive team gets the ball.

Uniforms and Equipment

A football player wears protective equipment under his uniform to prevent injuries.

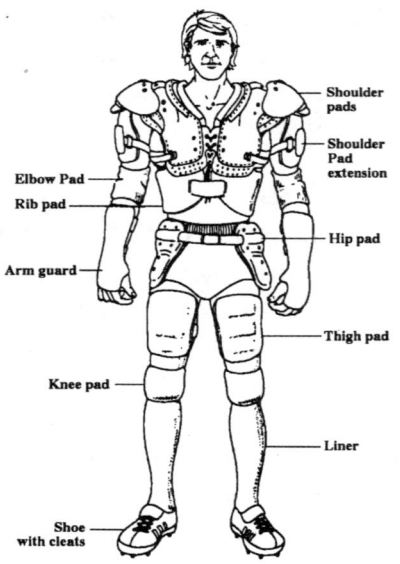

A typical football player's "protection."

The uniform is made of cotton or nylon. It consists of a shirt (called a *jersey*) and pants that end just below the knee. In most cases, thigh pads and knee pads are sewn into the pants. The uniforms fit tightly so that opposing players cannot grab them when trying to make a tackle.

The uniform is worn over all the padding, topped off by a helmet.

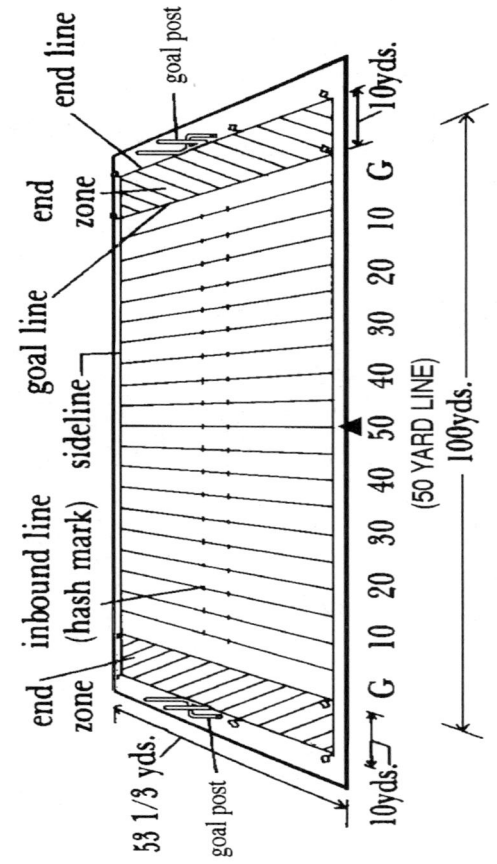

end line

goal post

end zone

goal line

sideline

inbound line (hash mark)

end zone

53 1/3 yds.

goal post

10yds.

10yds.

G   10   20   30   40   50   40   30   20   10   G

(50 YARD LINE)

100yds.

8

The Field

Football is played on a rectangular field of grass or artificial turf. The field of play is 100 yards long and 53 1/3 yards wide. At each end of the field is a goal line, followed by an end zone which is 10 yards deep.

The football field is divided in half. At the center is the *50-yard line*. Because of the way the field is marked, there are two 40-yard lines, two 30-yard lines, etc. A team tries to move the ball from its own half of the field into the opponent's territory and past the goal line.

At the back of each end zone is a goal post. The crossbar (which is 10 feet high and horizontal to the ground) and the two uprights form the target the kicker aims for when he attempts to kick extra points and field goals.

The goal post

How the Game Works

The football game begins with a kickoff at the 35-yard line. (Kickoffs also occur at the start of the second half and after a team scores a touchdown or a field goal.)

The receiving (or offensive) team then attempts to advance the ball down the field using passing and running plays.

In addition to receiving a kickoff, a team can gain possession of the ball in these ways:

  • The ball is fumbled (dropped) in the field of play and a defensive player picks it up or falls on it.

Tackling is a basic defensive skill. Defensive players use their shoulders and arms to stop an opposing player by bringing him to the ground.

Passing the football is one of two ways the offensive team can move the ball forward. The other method of advancing the ball down the field is to run with it.

• A defensive player *intercepts* a pass (catches a pass intended for an offensive player) while on the field of play.

• The offense doesn't move the ball at least 10 yards in four downs (plays).

• The defense receives (catches) a punt. (When the offense fails to gain a first down and is too far away to attempt a field goal, it usually punts.)

A defensive player cannot grab the ball away from the ball carrier after an official (one of the guys in the black and white striped shirts) blows the whistle to stop the play.

What Are Downs?

The offense doesn't get to keep the ball unless it can continue to move it down the field toward the goal line. The offensive team has four plays to move the ball at least 10 yards. Each play is called a *down*.

The first down is called *first and 10.* The 10 refers to how many yards the team must gain in order to get another first down. Let's say the offense runs the ball for six yards on its first play. After gaining six yards, the second play would be called

The down marker

second and four because it's the offensive team's second try, and it needs to gain four more yards for a first down. If it then gained three yards on "second and four," the next play would be *third and one.*

When the offense moves the ball for a first down within 10 yards of the opponent's goal line, it's called *first and goal*. Then the offense has four plays to score. (The offense can't get another first down, because there isn't enough playing field left to gain 10 more yards.)

Starting and Stopping Play

A play begins when the center (the man crouched over the ball) *hikes* or *snaps* the ball (hands it) to the quarterback. The quarterback always gets the ball first. He can then hand it off to another player, throw a pass to another player, or run with the ball himself.

Blocking is what an offensive player does to keep a defensive player from getting to the man with the ball. The blocker may use his shoulders or throw his body across a defender's legs.

Blocker

The play continues until one of the following events occurs:

- The player with the ball is tackled. (Somebody jumps on him, trips him, or otherwise causes him to fall down so his knee touches the ground.)
- The ball carrier steps out of bounds.
- A forward pass hits the ground before it is caught, or it is caught out of bounds.
- A runner's forward progress is stopped by the defensive team.
- A punted ball stops before a member of the receiving team touches it.
- A team scores.

Timing the Game

 Football is a timed game. One complete game is 60 minutes of actual playing time, divided into four periods (or quarters) of 15 minutes each. After two quarters are played, the players take a break during

halftime. During the game, the *game clock* keeps track of how much time is left in the period.

Because the game clock stops quite often, a 60-minute game can easily take three hours to complete.

The game clock is stopped whenever:

- The ball carrier runs out of bounds.
- A pass is thrown and not caught in bounds (a.k.a. an *incomplete pass*).
- A penalty is called, or an official calls a timeout.
- A team calls a timeout.
- Time runs out at the end of a quarter.
- A team scores.

The game clock continues to run:

- At the end of a running play.
- At the end of a successful passing play (as long as the ball stays in bounds).

Scoring Points

The only thing that really matters at the end of the game is which team scored the most points. That's how you tell the winner from the loser.

In the National Football League, there are four ways to score. Each is worth a specified number of points:

> **Touchdown — 6 points**
> **Field Goal — 3 points**
> **Safety — 2 points**
> **Point After Touchdown — 1 point**

We'll review each type of scoring, so you'll understand how each happens.

Touchdown

The most points a team can score on one play is six. This is called a touchdown. A touchdown is what happens when the offensive team (the team with the ball) crosses the opponent's goal line. It's what every team tries to do when it gets the ball.

A touchdown can occur:

- On a *running play*.
- On a *passing play* (when the offensive team's quarterback throws the ball to a player on his team, called a *receiver*).
- When a defensive team *intercepts* (catches) a pass intended for another player and runs it all the way past the goal line.
- When a team recovers a *fumble* (a dropped ball) in the opponent's end zone.

Field Goal

If a team can't advance the ball far enough to get a touchdown or a first down, it will often elect to try a *field goal*. A field goal has the second highest scoring value — three points.

To score a field goal, a *placekicker* has to kick the ball between the uprights of the goal post and up over the cross bar. No kicker is perfect, so a field goal is never a sure thing. But most kickers can consistently make field

Officials' Signals Used
When Points Are Scored

Touchdown (6 points), field goal (3 points), or a point after touchdown (1 point).

The signal for a safety (2 points).

goals of 30 yards or less, and they can kick 50-yard field goals about 50% of the time.

Virtually all field goal attempts are made on fourth down after a team has failed to gain enough yardage in three previous plays to get a first down. If the team is close enough to the goal, it usually attempts a field goal (otherwise, it will usually elect to punt).

Safety

A *safety* is the only way a team can score without having the ball. It is an unusual play that occurs when the defensive team tackles the ball carrier in his own end zone. The defensive team is awarded two points — and it also receives the ball after the offensive team punts from its own 20-yard line.

Point After Touchdown

After a touchdown, the placekicker tries to kick the ball through the uprights from about the 10-yard line. When he succeeds, and he usually does, the team scores one more point.

Players and
Positions

Each NFL team has 45 active players on its roster, but not everyone plays every game. In fact, there are plenty of players who get paid handsomely for standing around, *not* playing. These back-up players suddenly become important if a first-string player becomes injured and can no longer play.

In the early days of football, players used to play both offense and defense. Today, players' roles are more specialized, and most play either offense *or* defense. (This is sometimes called the *two platoon* system.) This way, each player is able to play the position he is best at.

During the game, the coach freely substitutes players between plays. Player substitutions enable players to get much-needed rest during the game.

Offense

The *offensive team* is the team with the ball. Likewise, the players who play when their team has the ball are called *offensive players.* The job of the offensive players is to move the ball down the field past the goal line. They work as a team, each performing certain specific tasks.

Possession of the ball is about 95 percent of winning the game, simply because the team that controls the ball has the most chances to score. The offensive players who handle the ball and score the points — quarterbacks, running backs, and receivers — are typically the game's superstars. Because of their popularity, they are usually the highest paid players on the field.

Offensive Line

The offensive players who do not, as a rule, handle the ball are called *offensive line-*

men . Offensive linemen are big, beefy men who *block* (push, shove) the defensive players out of the way so the player with the ball can gain some yardage by running or throwing the ball. They are not the most glamorous players in the game, but a great offensive line is the key to a great football team.

The offensive linemen play right on the line of scrimmage. The *center* lines up over the ball and hikes it to the quarterback. On either side of him are *guards,* and next to the guards are *tackles.* After the center snaps the ball, these five guys block like crazy.

On either side of the two tackles are *ends.* (They're called ends because they line up on the end of the line). When an end lines up right next to the tackle, he's called a *tight end.* When an end lines up away from the tackle, he's called a *split end* (or *wide receiver).* Unlike the other offensive linemen, ends can legally catch passes thrown to them by the quarterback.

Quarterback

The *quarterback* is the primary ball handler. He receives the snap from center, then he either passes it or hands it off to another player. He's the offensive player in charge, and he must make quick decisions while avoiding 300-pound guys who are trying to tear his head off.

Receivers and Running Backs

The guys who catch the passes thrown by the quarterback are called *receivers*. *Wide receivers* line up "wide" (away) from the interior linemen.

The guys who line up behind (and to the side) of the quarterback are called *running backs*. They get the hand-off from the quarterback and then run like heck. Running backs also catch short passes called *screen passes*, which are passes caught behind the line of scrimmage. Screen passes are used for short yardage gains and when the quarterback needs someone to throw to, *fast!*

Player Positions

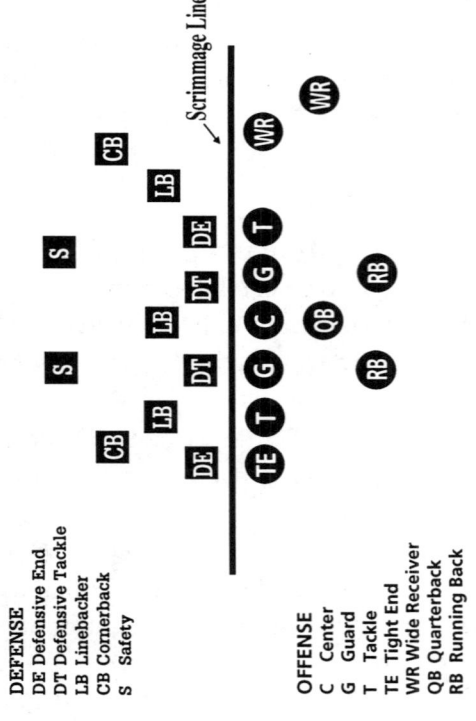

DEFENSE
DE Defensive End
DT Defensive Tackle
LB Linebacker
CB Cornerback
S Safety

OFFENSE
C Center
G Guard
T Tackle
TE Tight End
WR Wide Receiver
QB Quarterback
RB Running Back

24

Defense

The offensive players may get the big bucks, but it's the defense that really wins football games.

Although there are lots of different defensive formations, the defensive team has three basic types of players.

The Linemen

The 12-eggs-for-break-fast players on the defensive team are the linemen. They start on the line of scrimmage, right across from the offensive linemen.

The offensive linemen are huge because they try to protect the quarterback and block for the running backs; the defensive linemen are huge — even humongous — because their job is to get *past* the offensive linemen and tackle the ball carrier.

The traditional defense uses four linemen. From left to right, they're called *left end*, *left tackle, right tackle*, and *right end*. Sometimes there are just three linemen — two ends and a middle player called a *nose guard* or *nose tackle*. (He lines up "nose-to-nose" with the offensive team's center.)

Defensive linemen rush the quarterback on passing plays. When they tackle him before he throws the ball it's called a *sack*. A sack is such a big deal that the defensive lineman who sacks a quarterback usually does a victory dance of some kind.

Linemen also attempt to tackle the running backs as they dart through the line of scrimmage. Both sacks and tackles are official statistics, and they are the measuring sticks for defensive line performance.

Linebackers

The players in the center of the defensive formation are the *linebackers* — they back up the defensive linemen. If there are three, they're called *left linebacker, middle linebacker* and *right linebacker*. If there are

four, they're called *left outside linebacker,
left inside linebacker, right inside linebacker,*
and *right outside linebacker.*

Linebackers are probably the most versa-
tile defensive players. They have to be strong
enough to fend off blockers and tackle the
ball carrier. But they also have to be quick
and agile enough to defend against short
passing plays. It's a tough position, and the
best linebackers make a lot of tackles.

Defensive Backs

The last line of defense for the defensive
team is the *defensive backfield.* If the running
back makes it past the linemen and the linebackers, the only players who can prevent a
touchdown are the *defensive backs.*

Defensive backs are the smallest and fastest of the defensive players because their
primary job is to defend against long passing
plays. They "cover" the receivers who run
downfield, attempting to knock the ball away
when it comes — or even better, attempting

to intercept it. Defensive backs need quick reflexes, great timing, and tremendous instincts.

Normally there are two *cornerbacks* (left and right) who line up behind the linebackers. The two *safeties* are positioned in between and, usually, behind the cornerbacks. Safeties are the last line of defense in the backfield.

A *man-to-man defense* means that each of the defensive backs is covering a specific re-

ceiver. In a *zone defense,* each defensive back is responsible for a specific area of the field. An area where two zones overlap is called a *seam,* and often that's where the quarterback will try to throw a pass.

One of the most exciting plays in football happens when a defensive back intercepts a pass and runs it in for a touchdown. It's the biggest — and most dramatic— turnaround in the game.

Special Teams

The special teams players come onto the field for punts, kickoffs, field goals, and points after touchdowns.

Most of these players are *only* used for special teams. Because they're in the game for just one play at a time, they're often willing to risk major bodily harm just to make a tackle and impress the coach. These are the game's "kamikaze" players.

Special teams players include kickoff return specialists and punt returners — as well as players who are good offensive blockers and defensive tacklers.

Punting the ball.

The kicker and the punter are special teams players with very crucial roles. Many games are won — and lost — by kickers.

Penalties and Signals

Because football is a rough, physical game, many of the penalties the officials call are intended to keep players from getting hurt. For example, because a quarterback is the most vulnerable player, it is against the rules to hit him below the knees if the defender has a clear path for a sack. (See page 26.)

Football requires teams to move the ball forward toward the opponent's goal line in order to score. Consequently, the penalty for most rule violations is to move the ball backwards a specified number of yards. In some cases, the penalty also involves the loss of a down.

The following pages focus on the most common penalties plus the other signals that officials use during the game. (See also the officials' signals for scoring on page 18.)

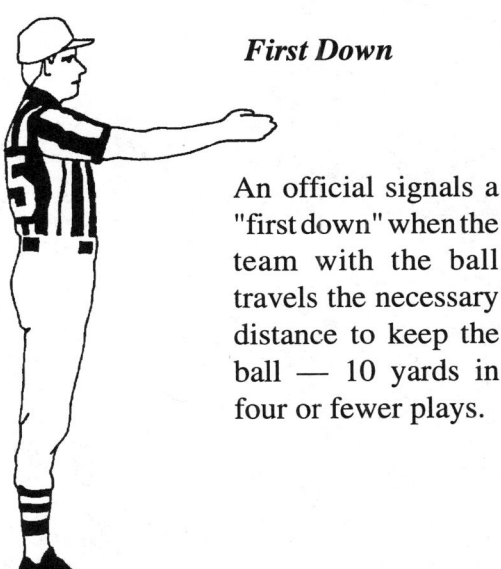

First Down

An official signals a "first down" when the team with the ball travels the necessary distance to keep the ball — 10 yards in four or fewer plays.

The signalling motion starts with the official's right arm extended upward. He then makes a "karate chop" motion and fully extends his arm forward.

False Start

Offside or Encroachment

Offensive player crossing the scrimmage line before the ball is snapped.
(Signal: forearms rotated over and over in front of body.)
Penalty: 5 yards.

Defensive player in the "neutral zone" (encroachment) or crossing the scrimmage line (offside) before the ball is snapped.
(Signal: hands on hips.)
Penalty: 5 yards.

Holding

Illegal Use of Hands

Offensive player grasping an opponent with the hands. (Signal: Grasping one wrist, the fist clenched, in front of chest.) Penalty: 10 yards.

Defensive player grasping an opponent. (Signal: Grasping one wrist, the hand open and facing forward,) Penalty: 5 yards and automatic first down.

Pass Interference

Personal Foul

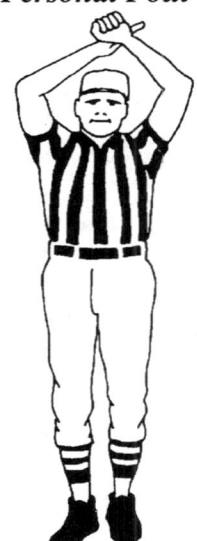

Hindering a receiver's (offense) or defender's (defense) attempt to catch a pass.
(Signal: Hands open and extended forward.)
Penalty: Varies.

Used for a variety of fouls, including clipping, roughing the passer and roughing the kicker.
(Signal: One wrist striking the other above the head)

Penalty Declined, Incomplete Pass, or Missed Field Goal/ Extra Point.

(Signal: Hands shifted back and forth in front of waist.)

More About Penalties

• When an official signals a penalty, he makes the motion for the particular violation, then points to the guilty team. (So, you can always tell which team has been called for the penalty.)

• Inside the 20-yard-line, most penalties which would move the ball toward the goal are assessed "half the distance to the goal line."

• A team can *decline* a penalty called on the opposition. For example, the offensive team will usually decline a penalty if it gained more yardage on the play than the penalty would give it.

35

NFL Teams and Conferences

There are 28 teams in the National Football League (NFL), 14 in each conference. Each team plays 16 games, including two against each team in its own division. Before the regular season, each team also plays four pre-season games.

American Football Conference (AFC)

Eastern Division
Buffalo Bills
Indianapolis Colts
Miami Dolphins
New England Patriots
New York Jets

Central Division
Cincinnati Bengals
Cleveland Browns
Houston Oilers
Pittsburgh Steelers

Western Division
Denver Broncos
Kansas City Chiefs
Los Angeles Raiders
San Diego Chargers
Seattle Seahawks

National Football Conference (NFC)

Eastern Division
Dallas Cowboys
New York Giants
Philadelphia Eagles
Phoenix Cardinals
Washington Redskins

Central Division
Chicago Bears
Detroit Lions
Green Bay Packers
Minnesota Vikings
Tampa Bay Buccaneers

Western Division
Atlanta Falcons
Los Angeles Rams
New Orleans Saints
San Francisco 49ers

The Road to the Super Bowl

After the regular season, the team with the best won-lost record in each division is the division champion. The three division champions from each conference, plus the three nondivision champions with the best records ("wild card" teams) enter the playoffs. Teams advance through the playoffs as long as they keep winning. Ultimately, the surviving NFC team meets the remaining AFC team in the Super Bowl in January.

Game Strategy

One of the reasons football is such a popular spectator sport is because winning a game involves a tremendous amount of strategy. And the foundation of virtually all football strategy comes down to one thing: controlling possession of the ball.

A team can't score without the ball (except when it tackles an opposing ball carrier in the end zone for a safety — which doesn't happen often.) Therefore, the best football teams are those which can consistently keep the ball by moving it down the field.

Running plays are the best way to do this. A good running back always protects the ball from his tacklers, making a fumble unlikely. Running plays are also the best way to *run out the clock*. (Remember, unless the runner goes out of bounds or a team calls a timeout, the game clock keeps running after a player has been tackled.) That's why you'll see teams which are out in front near the end of the game calling nothing but running plays. Quite simply, the team wants the game to be over so it can collect its win and go home.

Passing plays, on the other hand, are the fastest way to advance the ball down the field. When a team is desperately trying to score near the end of a game, you'll see it throw passes almost exclusively. An incomplete pass stops the game clock, so it enables the team to regroup and call another play without using up valuable *game time*.

"Hurry-Up" or "Two-Minute" Offense

Two minutes before the end of each playing half is an official's timeout called the *two-minute warning*. If a team is in need of a score, it will often run its *hurry-up* or *two-minute offense*. This type of offense uses short passing plays in which the receiver catches the ball and runs out of bounds to stop the clock. (One of the marks of a great quarterback is the ability to run an effective hurry-up offense that results in points being scored.)

Teams will often save all of their three timeouts per half, just in case they need them during their two-minute offense.

"Run and Shoot" Offense

Traditionally, football teams have emphasized running plays. (Some people call this *power* football.) But the latest trend is toward a more wide-open style that uses far more passing. This style is called the *run and shoot* offense, and it requires a talented quarterback and many fast receivers.

Even though they are exciting to watch, many *run and shoot* teams have trouble controlling the ball and running out the clock. Consequently, most football purists still have their doubts about the effectiveness of this type of offensive strategy.

Understanding
Football Statistics

They're called box scores. Printed in every newspaper sports section in America on Mondays during football season, they are a shorthand way of capturing the most important information about a game. But unless you know how to translate them, box scores are absolutely meaningless.

On the next page is an actual NFL game box score. Here's what it means:

❶ The final score of the game.

❷ Scoring by quarters:

Atlanta   7 0 14 10—31

means that Atlanta scored 7 points in the first quarter, 0 in the second, 14 in the third and 10 in the fourth — for a total of 31 points.

❸ Scoring plays, each quarter. For example:

Chi— Anderson 49 run (Butler kick), 4:05

means that Chicago scored a touchdown on a 49-yard run by Anderson after 4 minutes and

Here's a typical football box score from a newspaper.

NFL SUMMARIES

❶ BEARS 41, FALCONS 31

❷ Atlanta	7 0 14 10—31	
Chicago	17 14 7 3—41	

❸ **First Quarter:** Chi—Anderson 49 run (Butler kick), 4:05; Chi—FG Butler 20, 10:39; Chi—Waddle 41 pass from Harbaugh (Butler kick), 13:10; Atl—Rison 71 pass from Miller (Johnson kick), 13:33. **Second Quarter:** Chi—Anderson 14 run (Butler kick), 7:25; Chi—Davis 11 pass from Harbaugh (Butler kick), 13:17. **Third Quarter:** Atl—Rison 6 pass from Miller (Johnson kick), 4:49; Atl—Jones 23 pass from Miller (Johnson kick), 8:30; Chi—Muster 14 run (Butler kick), 12:57. **Fourth Quarter:** Atl—FG Johnson 46, 4:35; Chi—FG Butler 21, 9:04; Atl—Rison 10 pass from Miller (Johnson kick), 15:00. **A**—63,528.

	Atl	Chi
❹ First downs	19	23
Rushes-yards	10-24	36-217
Passing	324	272
Return Yards	5	10
❺ Comp-Att-Int	30-48-1	18-24-0
❻ Sacked-Yards Lost	3-27	2-8
Punts	4-45	4-43
Fumbles-Lost	0-0	0-0
Penalties-Yards	3-34	7-91
Time of Possession	25:21	34:39

INDIVIDUAL STATISTICS

❼ **RUSHING**—Atlanta, Broussard 5-21, Miller 1-4, Pegram 1-1, Fulhage 1-0, T.Smith 2-(minus 2). Chicago, Muster 10-96, Anderson 15-74, Harbaugh 5-21, Davis 1-21, Green 2-3, Lewis 3-2.

❽ **PASSING**—Atlanta, Miller 30-48-1-351. Chicago, Harbaugh 18-24-0-280.

❾ **RECEIVING**—Atlanta, Rison 10-177, Hill 8-83, Pritchard 8-52, T.Jones 3-41, Hinton 1-(minus 2). Chicago, Anderson 6-80, Waddle 3-62, Muster 3-51, Jennings 2-25, Wright 1-24, Blackwell 1-18, Davis 1-11, Lewis 1-9.

42

5 seconds were played in the first quarter. Butler kicked the extra point.

Chi— FG Butler 20; 10:39

means that Butler kicked a 20-yard field goal 10 minutes and 39 seconds into the first quarter.

❹ Rushes-yards   10-24

is the number of running plays (10) by Atlanta and the total yards gained on those plays (24).

❺ Comp-Att-Int   30-48-1

means that Atlanta completed 30 passes during the game out of 48 attempts, and 1 was intercepted.

❻ Punts   4-45

Atlanta punted 4 times during the game, averaging 45 yards per punt.

❼ RUSHING— Atlanta, Broussard 5-21

Broussard carried the ball 5 times, gaining a total of 21 yards.

❽ PASSING— Atlanta, Miller 30-48-1-351

30 passes completed out of 48 attempted by Miller; 1 interception; 351 total yards gained.

❾ RECEIVING— Atlanta, Rison 10-177

Rison caught 10 passes, gaining 177 total yards.

Football Trivia
(To Impress Your Friends)

Any self-respecting football fan knows a fair amount of football trivia — facts, figures and famous players. Here's a quick list of "important" football facts.

1. Teams with the best Super Bowl records: San Francisco 49ers and Pittsburgh Steelers are both 4-0.

2. Teams with the worst Super Bowl records: Denver Broncos and Minnesota Vikings are both winless in four attempts (0-4).

3. The most-watched television show of all time: Super Bowl XXVII (January 31, 1993). watched by 133.4 million Americans. Score: Dallas Cowboys 52, Buffalo Bills 17.

4. All-time rushing leader: Walter Payton, Chicago Bears ('75-'87) — 16,726 yards.

5. Single season rushing leader: Eric Dickerson, L.A. Rams ('84) — 2,105 yards.

44

6. All-time passing leader: Fran Tarkenton, Minn. Vikings-NY Giants ('61-'78) — 47,003 yards.

7. Single season passing leader: Dan Marino, Miami Dolphins ('84) — 5,084 yards.

8. All-time pass receiving — total yards gained: James Lofton, Green Bay-L.A. Raiders-Buffalo ('78-'92) — 13,821 and counting.

9. All-time pass receiving — number of receptions: Art Monk, Washington Redskins ('80-'92) — 847 and counting.

10. Most consecutive games with a pass reception: Steve Largent, Seattle ('77-'89) — 177.

11. Most seasons in NFL: George Blanda, Chicago Bears-Baltimore-Houston-Oakland ('49-75) — 26 seasons.

12. Most points scored — career: George Blanda, ('49-75) — 2,002 points.

13. Number of teams playing in domed stadiums: 7 (Houston, Detroit, New Orleans, Seattle, Minnesota, Indianapolis, Atlanta).

14. Most consecutive games lost: Tampa Bay ('76-'77) — 26.

Glossary of
Football Terms

backfield — offensive players who line up behind the line of scrimmage.

blitz — a defensive play in which linebackers, cornerbacks and/or safeties charge across the line of scrimmage in an effort to sack the quarterback.

bomb — a long forward pass.

draw play — a running play in which the quarterback drops back as if to throw a pass, then hands the ball to a running back.

extra point (point after touchdown) — the one-point kicking play that follows a touchdown.

fair catch — an unhindered catch of a punt or kickoff. Must be signaled by raising a hand.

field goal — a three-point play scored when a kick goes over the crossbar and between the uprights of the goal post.

field position — the location of the ball. Good field position is near the opponent's goal line. Bad field position is near one's own goal line.

first down — a team has four downs (plays) in which to gain 10 yards. When it does, a first down is earned, giving the team four more plays.

fumble — unintentionally dropping the ball.

hash marks — the two short lines which intersect each five-yard line toward the middle of the field, used to position the ball for a new play.

interception — a pass caught by a defensive player.

line of scrimmage — an imaginary line which extends from the forward tip of the ball to both sidelines. Offensive and defensive players must stay on their side of the line until the ball is snapped.

neutral zone —the area between the offensive and defensive lines, the length of the football in width.

overtime — if the score is tied after four quarters of play, an extra period is played until one team scores. If neither team scores in overtime, the game ends in a tie. (Playoff games continue with additional overtime periods until a team scores.)

penalty flag — a yellow flag thrown by an official when he spots a rules violation. (For more on penalties, see pages 30-35.)

prevent defense — an alignment using extra defensive backs to prevent long passes.

roll-out — a passing play in which the quarterback runs a short distance behind the line of scrimmage before throwing the ball.

rushing play — an offensive running play.

rushing the passer — an attempt by a defensive player to tackle the quarterback.

sack — tackling the quarterback before he can throw a pass.

safety — tackling a ball carrier in his own end zone, scoring two points for the defensive team. The defensive team then receives the ball after offensive team punts from its own 20-yard line.

screen pass — an offensive play in which the quarterback tosses a short pass to a receiver waiting behind a "wall" of blockers.

sideline — the out-of-bounds line on each side of the field.

touchback — receiving a kickoff, punt, or intercepting a pass in one's own end zone, and electing not to advance it. The next play begins from the 20-yard line.

touchdown — a six-point score that occurs when the ball is advanced across the opponent's goal line.